GW00838700

The Wilds
An Anthology

First published September 2007
by Ek Zuban
c/o 52 Carlow Street
Middlesbrough
TS1 4SD
United Kingdom

www.ekzuban.co.uk
www.myspace.com/ekzuban

Edited by Bob Beagrie & Andy Willoughby

ISBN 978-0-9553930-2-0

Cover design by Kitch-en from original artwork by Gail Henderson
'Dipping The Heel'. Layout by Kitch-en www.kitch-en.co.uk

This publication has been made possible through the support of Arts
Council England North East. Ek Zuban also acknowledges support from
Middlesbrough Borough Council, and Tees Valley Arts.

Ek Zuban is a member of the Independent Northern Publishers.
www.northernpublishers.co.uk

Foreword

The Wilds Anthology brings together the work of established and emerging poets from the North East of England who worked together as mentors and mentees, exploring the theme of geographic, natural, urban, social and psychological wildernesses.

The editors invited fifteen established poets to work with a promising poet they had come across through various courses, projects or who had become a regular contributor to *KENAZ* magazine (a cutting edge magazine dedicated to providing the first step on the publishing ladder for talented new writers from the Tees Valley). The mentors selected two of the mentee's four submitted poems to focus on and guide their mentee through a process of reflection and rewriting. They then submitted the final pieces along with one poem of their own that had been inspired by their mentee or which explored the general theme.

In *The Wilds* you will find poems that are edgy and unsafe, that stalk the boundaries, poems that won't sit compliantly on the page but bristle like the coat of a wolf or a feral cat at an uneasy scent carried on a night wind. There are also quieter reflective poems where the poet's mind moves upon silence like Yeats' long legged fly. You'll find stark contrasts and startling connections between the poems and many of them deal with difficult subjects. What you won't find here are the same old-same-old-poems that are obviously well crafted and refined but have lost the vitality and vibrant energy of raw articulation of direct experience in an attempt to comply to the narrow aesthetics of the literary elite who dominate much of the U.K.'s mainstream poetry publishing.

By combining work by established and new writers and allowing the mentor's poem to act as an introduction to the work of each mentee we hope to bring attention to the vast potential of North East talent that is often obscured from a wider public. We also hope this anthology provides a stepping stone towards further visibility and recognition for the new writers involved, while giving a valuable snapshot of some of the most exciting voices in the North East, from Teesside to Tyneside. *The Wilds* is a map to guide you to literary delights and new adventures, but tread carefully, 'HERE BE DRAGONS.'

You can buy further work by each of the mentor poets from the Independent Northern Publishers' website on www.northernpublishers.co.uk
Check out *KENAZ* magazine and our other publications on
www.ekzuban.co.uk and www.myspace.com/ekzuban

Contents

Gordon Hodgeon Introduces Gary Ming

Gordon Hodgeon was born in Lancashire in 1941.He has worked in schools, in teacher education and in educational administration. From 1972 to 1996 he was a schools' adviser in Teesside. He has been active for many years in NATE, in Northern Arts, Cleveland Arts and New Writing North. These days he helps run Mudfog Press. Publications include *November Photographs* (1981), *A Cold Spell* (1996) and *Winter Breaks* (Smokestack Books, 2006). He has twice won the Mirehouse Poetry Prize. Gordon is a member of Brotton Writers and Hall Garth Poets.

'Gary and I worked on his poems by email. We couldn't manage a meeting and this 'distance' mode worked well, though it probably helped that we knew each other. Email exchange allows sharp focus on the text. It might have been a problem, as it set Gary's free-rein writing approach smack up against my obsessive eye for detail. We worked on all four poems; Gary dropped one and I chose these two, mainly for contrast. *Passenger* conveys a hallucinogenic landscape which is out there and in here as well. A terrifying journey – you are both torn away and left abandoned. *On the News* is a tender poem which counterpoints the gamble of passion with the logic of sense, exactly catching the precarious transfer of love's immediacy into the shared life of a child. The poem realises the fragility, does not put aside the surrounding wilderness. Did the mentoring bring the poems on? Yes, because Gary was strong enough to take what he wanted from the exchange and to react positively to my questions and quibbles by making his own revisions.'

Gary Ming is Middlesbrough born, mixed blood, first published by Mudfog Press in a pamphlet called *Give it a Try*, has since been published in *KENAZ* magazine. He has performed his poems at The Hydrogen Jukebox and has been involved in previous mentoring schemes with Andy Croft and Bob Beagrie.

'Working with Gordon gave me a greater insight in remaining objective when editing a poem of my own. The benefit of Gordon's experience is hopefully evident in the reading.'

Over The Border

I'm looking for the Customs House
the old one, the way we were
before the transformation.

       The river's invisible, licks
       along down there, hums its burden
       under crane feet, abstractions of the cranium,
       glass-and-chrome emporia, o my *Boro Nova*,
       an old cat sniffing out to the North Sea,
       an old-fashioned stink to it.

Still looking for it, are you, the old one, the Customs House?
It isn't the Riverside, the stadium, all girder legs in a can-can?
Not the Transporter where the cars fly slow, traditional like
cargoes of iron ore, dogs' breath, slave-sweat, Serb girls, soft drugs, hard core?
Are you late for a meeting?

He doesn't know it, the Customs House,
he's new like the rest of us,
attacks the taxi he's repairing with a very large hammer,
doesn't know where it or Middlesbrough
or England is, only works here over the border, made it
to a street of car parts, brick caverns, spare dogs. In a white van
two men open their windows waiting for the boatman
who hasn't a clue, might have gone anywhere, if you
enquire at the metal box there, the window, the sign
on the door.
              – SECURITASK–

Trail two left legs through puddles, over rust heaps,
by old tyres, could have laid me down, could have
cried
my one life, you don't need to read
The Cut-and-Paste Land, the bits you need on a shore
are
the ruins, the illegal, the guard dog, the lingo, the raw stuff, the rusty sex,
the trespass, the trespass, the forgive us
who are late for our meeting, forgive us.

Oh has it a tower to poke at the clouds, to video

2

the visitors?
You can't see it from here, like.

Metal sheet doorways, plastic blind window shields,
green flickering laughter of mudland where *ex cathedral* stood.
– RCIP–

Press the empty button, the enter yard, the gate says, the voice slides
and trips out the Customs House, the old one, the Excise, the Excuse,
the Hack Me Out, the Stab Me In, the new land you found it

all the lines cleared to the drop off the flat world.

On the News

Perhaps I'm the romantic,
dealing with links, bonds,
futures and dreams.

You,
your logic strong-arms
me into submission
pounds, cents, dollars, pence
level-headed sense.

Little left of the girl
who gambled futures
that first night unfolding
of each other.

I,
buy books on
vitamins, diets
plan names. Set dates
for a craft that might
carry us to old age.

You fan a sheaf of dollar bills
slap my foolish head away.
Now that's that!

Passenger

Eyes missing concrete pull
a furrowed brow
the sun shrinks behind orange
clouds pocking the sky,
bruising hills purple.
Endless fields click with
cateye regularity
mnemonic head banging
in this metal box

Eyes missing tarmac falter,
a crow trampolines from a pylon,
laughingly circles a spire offering
no sanctuary, then dots
to the horizon.

A fence snakes, constricts
chokes and contains convicts
from each other and the
distant villages where nothing
happens nothing changes
night and day night and day.

Eyes missing life widen,
fridge white walls scream
a scratched fuck you!

Hopes and iron-ware
drag wrists and dreams
to the floor.

Marilyn Longstaff Introduces Rebecca Severi

Marilyn Longstaff lives in Darlington; member of Vane Women, the writing, performing and publishing collective; Arts Council 'Northern Promise Award' (2003); published in a range of magazines, in anthologies, and on the Web; first pamphlet *Puritan Games* (Vane Women Press, 2001); full collection, *Sitting Among the Hoppers* (Arrowhead Press, 2004).

'Both Rebecca's and my own poems are concerned with landscapes; Rebecca's poems reflect on the pull of the unfamiliar, and the mixture of fear and exhilaration that this provokes. My poem wrestles with a landscape that has become unfamiliar and dangerous, through weather and foolhardiness. Both refer to the presence of a known other, and have hints of the familiar, which render the wild experiences manageable. Both are in free verse, but the different forms that the poets have chosen to impose on them allow for that balance between order and chaos, between wild and tameable.'

Rebecca Severi is 23, lives in Middlesbrough and works in a library. She has previously published poetry in *KENAZ* magazine and was a founder member of The Hydrogen Jukebox Cabaret in Darlington performing poetry, original songs and acting in pieces for voices by well-known North-East poets. She was previously mentored by Jo Colley for Tees Valley Arts Writing In Action programme and has studied Creative Writing and Research with Bob Beagrie at The University of Teesside. Her other influences are Angela Carter, William Carlos Williams, Charles Bukowski and the Finnish contemporary beat poets Kalle Niinikangas, Tapani Kinnunen and Esa Hirvonen. She is also deeply interested in and inspired by Silent Cinema particularly the work and life of Mary Pickford. She says of the mentoring process...

"It was really interesting being mentored by Marilyn. It was fascinating to debate the use of a word or phrase and it really made me think about the form and meanings of my poems. Whether I did or didn't take a particular piece of advice she always helped me think about what it was that I really wanted to say and get a greater sense of my own voice in poetry."

Pilgrimage
for Jackie

Beyond the false calm of Muker car park and
Level paths across set-aside meadows –
Indulgent lying-in, under snow blankets – we reach
Zs of the River Swale in blast valley,
Zero tolerance for fools who've ventured out.
Angry landscape, it lashes us, unleashes furious
Rods of iced-venom, funnelled and shot
Down this tunnel of doom.

Silent and intrepid, we press on towards Kisdon.
No shelter
Our heads lowered to shield cheeks from
Weather beating. The gale is
Shouting, but we are deaf in our stupidity,
Neither willing to be the first to give in.
Oligarchs of the State of Stubbornness,
We press on. A man with dog

Stumbles out of the white-out,
Laughs, "It's wild in there."
Extreme cold.
Extreme wet.
The full force of 'March wind doth blow'

Straight at us.
No shelter, no turning back, with
Only the possibility of sandwiches to sustain us,
We press on.

As we climb past abandoned lead mine,
Reach the top, the clouds lift
And the sun seduces my packed lunch,
Your flask, from sodden rucksacks.
Only one bite, one sip, be-
Fore you glance behind.

So, that was that then. Purple
Night is racing towards us again. Break
Over, food thrown back into packs,

We press on through blizzard and
Dee ee eep drifts, down, down to cross the falls.
Rushing, we lose the way. On the far bank,
Inch up treacherous snow and ice cliff,
Floundering,
Thigh deep, but determined we won't turn back. We

Struggle to high path and dry interval,
Lounge on a tree-trunk-seat for delayed snack.
It's decision time – the sky track,
Ploughing into cloud, or the
Safer route? We go for the
Lower. On the home stretch now, we wind
In and out of snow pockets on this
Dark side that holds no homesteads,
Each relieved to have reached the

Turn, we wallow in hallucinations of dry feet,
Escapist dreams of mythical tea rooms
And crackling fires, honey; we need to
Run as it grows yet darker,
Or we'll miss this chintz antithesis.
On our knees like pilgrims, we
    Make it – last orders for tea and scones.

After The Sauna

After the walk around the island
far away from the grind of work,

Feel of the forest footpath:
Scratchy pine needles.

In this place
long socks protect

white ungainly legs
from insidious ticks

You chop wood for the sauna fire
stripped to the waist like Grizzly Adams.

I sip at the bear label brew,
electric fridge our luxury.

The spit of the coals as you ladle on water,
peeling off my steam soaked bikini.

Then knee deep in the rain splashed Baltic
pressured to show I'm a worthy woods-girl

Like no Finn after the sauna –
afraid of drowning in choppy water.

We lay pink and naked on the mattress
cleansed by steam, full of cold beer

outside toilet standing distant –
pissing in a blue bucket at night.

"Sail away with me honey..."

In Finland on a small island,
sun-warmed rocks under bare feet,
enjoying cd's, drinking Karhu.

A slight breeze carries
the smell of Finnish sausage
you slow cook on the Grilli.

Out of sight in shadow,
fish are swishing,
flapping,
stirring up muddy reed beds.

In the near distance
little red boathouse
hidden by a passing ship's bow -

wonder where it's going,
imagine being caught up
in the rolling tail of its wake.

Jo Colley Introduces Ellie Grassick

Jo Colley lives, works and writes in Darlington. Her first collection of poetry, *As If*, came out in 2001, published by Vane Women. *Punchdrunk*, a bi-lingual pamphlet with Finnish poet Esa Hirvonen, came out in 2005, published by Ek Zuban. Her next collection, *Weeping for The Lovely Phantoms*, is due out later this year, this time with Salt. She is closely involved in the spoken word life of the region, having been co-director of Hydrogen Jukebox in Darlington for six years, and currently organising poetry events in Durham as part of Colpitts Poets. She likes to experiment with image, music and spoken word in her performances.

'Mentoring Ellie was not difficult. For a start, we have been working together for some time, as part of the Hydrogen Jukebox cabaret team. We have written together on various themes, including horror, fairy tales and religion, with impressive results. Ellie has an amazing vocabulary – she just knows loads of words. She also has a rich inner life in which Tim Burton wrestles with Stephen Gaimler. The move to Norwich and to a university course in which she can give reign to her vivid imagination and luscious use of language seems to be working well. I can see a new maturity in her work as she experiments with form and new themes.

We decided she would work on Half Waking and Orion, two contrasting poems: Orion is sharp, clean, controlled. Half Waking is more sensuous, meandering, erotic. Ellie worked on sharpening up a verse in Orion (which is the poem which inspired my own Star-gazing). Half Waking, by contrast, became longer, as she extended the tree metaphor, making it more a poem of transformation, but retaining its sensual feel. I think the result is poems which show two distinct aspects of her poetry writing talent.'

Ellie Grassick lived in Darlington for almost eight years. In between painting, drawing, writing and education, she was a member of a number of local and regional theatre groups, including the Castle Players and part of the cabaret team of The Hydrogen Jukebox. She is currently studying American Literature and Creative Writing at the University of East Anglia, where she enjoys TS Eliot, Edgar Allan Poe, fairytales, Northern Exposure, Jasper Fforde, hot chocolate, and lie-ins.

Star gazing

Why did we choose that night, after years of idle talk
to go out in search of meteorites? The line between us
worn so thin, I was hanging by a thread
above the void, suspended.

In the darkest spot we could find
we opened the sun roof, lay back
with our binoculars, swept the sky
like snipers, checking for movement.

Whilst we argued about time zones,
the names of constellations, which way is up,
the sky stealthily drew a soft grey veil
over her sequinned nakedness

deeming us unworthy to behold
the Leonides in flight. For a while
we scrutinised each cloud tear
longing for a glimpse, a flash, a spark.

Nothing but emptiness.
I drove you home,
returned to my cold house
falling, falling until I hit the earth.

Half Waking

We lie
sleep-furred
bodies twisted like tree-roots
warm and grown
layered deep
under soft, shrubbed sleep.
The wind moves to murmur
"At last, my love."
His fingers
trace the dips and hollows of my neck.
It is a wooded path
shadowed and brown
well-trodden, smoothed down
by the fingertips of feet.
Our affection pools
like rainwater,
sending new shoots slipping up fresh
amongst stilled lids
stiff leaves.
My collarbone is a root, old
and worn, it carves out a step,
slips under skin,
leaf-dappled and dim
and bending in the wind:
My hair,
swaying like branches
blown like willows
as the earth of his chest
moves in his breath-gale.
Warm in autumn-dream,
kisses like leaves
scatter love and leave
August and waking behind.
A whisper flutters
blossoming sweet
between the boughs of our
gnarled and carved
bedroom.
"My foxy darling..."

sleek-tailed and sly
soporific beside me
he slips his hand into mine.
So off we drift,
and make our den
in my sleeping wood.

Orion

. Orion is out
tonight, hunting the depths of
. a wooded blue sky

He draws, stretches taut
his bow of suns, burns cold heat
through his frosted limbs;

a wilderness of
clear, winter night, blanketing
me, and mine, and I –

I will sit with him
breath misting, feeling the hunt
wheel slowly above.

Tom Kelly Introduces Mel Bartliff

Tom Kelly's most recent poetry collection is, *The Wrong Jarrow* (Smokestack). Other publications include *John Donne in Jarrow* (Here Now); *Their Lives* (Tears in the Fence); *That Time of Life* (KT Publications) and *The Picture From Here* (Sand Publications).

He has written many plays and musicals including *Kelly* (with Alan Price); *The Machine Gunners, Dan Dare and Tom & Catherine* (John Miles) and *Steel Town* (Steve Thompson).

He is also part of the WMDJ team, with songwriter/producer Steve Thompson and photographer Peter Dixon that produced, VOICES, a multimedia exhibition, which is touring the north in 2007.

'I had four poems from Mel and felt immediately that these were not exercises in a creative writing class. These poems were borne out of experience. Here was a harsh life and Mel was trying to capture his world, in order to make sense of it. Two poems stood out. I paid attention to them and sent my comments. Mel took my ideas in a very positive way. More suggestions, amendments and telephone calls followed and I believe we have two poems both Mel and me can be proud of. Thanks Mel.'

Mel Bartliff was born and brought up in North Ormesby, Middlesbrough. The son of a steel worker in a long line of steel workers. He left school at the age of fifteen with nothing more than a rebellious rage against authority and an appreciation of the written word. After four years he severed the umbilical cord with the steel works, seeking the freedom enjoyed by the uncommitted. He began to write seriously just a few years ago as the first step on the long road back. He describes his work as 'from the streets', of which he is all too familiar.

Sunday In Winter

Rain drills his face,
beer's worn off.

The jukebox yawns light in the empty bar,
this is the worst of times:
afternoon stupor in dank bedrooms.

He watches from the upstairs window,
one slipper shoved on, the other in his hand, like a cosh,
he berates the wall
with his head, staggering with the shock
of the mess he's living in.

Things were better: children looked up to him,
his wife waited for his return...
Was that him?
Or some stranger's life rifled,
a pill that allowed a dream to sneak in,
filch its corrupt way into this unbearable aching.

Touch the Moon

Neon signs
tubular letters.
Plastic, shiny chrome,
coffee
thick white cups,
jukebox shaking the floor.
Loose rolled spliffs
under the table
and I float out of the door.

Punctured arm.
Liquid filth,
shadows threaten,
buildings tilt,
street lights spinning,
purple sky,
pavements rear:
flapping arms
I can fly.
Touch the moon.

Feral

I crouch on my gothic pile, yellow eye blinking
from this lofty, soot stained finger: survey my parish below.
Night reaches from the corners of day,
the mantle of my streets is changing
to the forgotten half of man's existence.

A distant mongrel courts the moon, his howling splits the air.
Beetle like taxis scuttle, ferrying eager cargo.
Shadows point: dead man's fingers,
cones of yellow from street lamps illuminate tainted puddles.

Badly wrapped bundles cough in shop doorways
isolated islands of darkness.
The rustle of town centre undergrowth, an eddying wind from the river,
knee trembling sex in an alley behind buildings carved out of coal.

The wail of urgent sirens echo against my stone
the searching eyes of a street girl reflecting the vulnerability of addiction.
A turmoil of mixed emotions, violence must settle the score:
a pathetic shoe in the gutter, a blood stained shirt supports a wall.
Muffled groans from a cardboard box, house of dreams, cave of despair.

The bone crunching stamp of a drunken boot,
muffled by chimes of protest,
a flock of bright coats attend a mill of flailing limbs:
the sobering click of handcuffs.

Vomit, blood, urine, legacy of the night.
Tired faces etched by neon, as the ebbing tide of night
drifts away and the feral cat waits her turn in my parish far below.

S.J. Litherland Introduces Nora Moe Graff

S.J. Litherland's latest collections include *The Homage* (Iron 2006) a sequence about former England cricket captain Nasser Hussain and *The Work of the Wind* (Flambard 2006) about her tumultuous years with fellow poet Barry MacSweeney who died in 2000. Previous collections: *The Apple Exchange* (Flambard 1999), *Flowers of Fever* (Iron 1992), *The Long Interval* (Bloodaxe 1986). She has received two Northern Writers' Awards. Her work has appeared in various anthologies, notably *The Forward Book of Poetry 2001*, the *Bloodaxe New Women Poets, North by North East* (Iron) and *Modern Poets of Northern England* (translated into Russian). She was co-editor of *The Poetry of Perestroika* (Iron) and has edited many books. Born in Warwickshire, she has lived in Durham City since 1965 and is a founding member of Vane Women writers' collective and Press and an organiser of Colpitts Poetry, which hosts poetry readings in the city.

'I thought the structure of the poems wasn't wild enough for the theme of the anthology. So I encouraged Nora to experiment with line indents, letting go of the left hand margin. I also thought that a few questions could be asked in 'The importance' as she said the journey left a question mark. In 'Advice' I suggested switching her first and second stanzas, and there was an interesting discussion over a couple of lines. I advised some small cuts and improved punctuation, but my most important contribution was to identify that she was using rhetorical lines among ordinary language and this gave her a distinctive style. We then had a correspondence about rhetorical language. Many poets use the device of mixing rhetoric with the vernacular; chief among them W.H. Auden. It can sound heavy but mixed with everyday speech it becomes imaginative and powerful.'

Nora Moe Graff started writing at 15 as an outlet for her thoughts. She is Norwegian but has always been drawn to the English language and is currently doing an exchange year in England where she has attended creative writing classes with W.N. Herbert at Newcastle University and has contributed to *KENAZ* magazine and performed at the launch events.

'Being part of The Wilds project with Jackie Litherland as my mentor has forced me to be more critical of my own writing. I have learned more about "carving" my work, as Ezra Pound would put it; to focus on the crucial part of my poem in order to arrive at the essence of what I wish to express.'

For Rachel

We're serving drinks
at our **Salon de Impropriété**
      The chopping in two has come to an end
the unexpected knife
      the martyrdom by arrows
the Apocalypse is on hold.
      Everything is scaled down

to the trying on of hats

the making of clothes
      the latest in stockings
half lace half fishnet

the **Emporium** is well lit
      the struggle of life
manifest.
      We've given up on what is divine

and taken up **shopping**.
      Such a relief
to take a rest
      and watch those boxes**!**
they're tipping over.
      Madam you may enter
with your pram and carrier bags.
      You have

a **purse.**
      We have triumphed over *Last Days*
and gone back to work.
      Now we must get busy.
You've come to join us. A momentous decision.
You've just walked away from the pavements
of **Lewisham**, the bargains and offers
      and come
to the **bazaar of Glamorous Outfits**.

of shoes   new outfit   bring bolts
of cloth, and this special hat
                              champagne

we digress

there's naked bathing and the party's
on.
        You can't *resist*
strolling in
        from shabby streets and plaster dust
and the daily grind.
        We're what you've lost!

Advice from a Stranger

                    I made myself small,
                        insignificant,
unworthy of attention.

Distressed by foul sounds
bellowed.

Passenger to passenger
giving birth to a wish
not to move, nor speak,
nor exchange looks,
                    least of all be noticed.

Old intimidates young,
man scares woman
with hair greasy
and mind seemingly gone.

                    This I have learned
                    about attention-craving people.
                    Never ignore them.
                    Pray you will be ignored.

A few rows ahead
the groaning continues,
and grows, expanding like a weed
pressing the beauty of the world aside
to nurture its own need.

The ravings of a madman.

                    But in the midst of all his misbehaving
                    he uttered these words of wisdom
                    (or was it merely a whisper
                    in my own haunted head?)

Remember your fears. Never mind me.

The importance of being the greatest distance runner in Gateshead

The journey left a question mark.

A story on a wall hidden in a clue,
a simple sentence and that was just it
too simple, too ordinary
to convey the pulse of art --
                                 a heartbeat in history.

A sentence must be read. It asks for it
so I did, half expecting a Biblical quote –
                                wisdom for life
or at least for that day
but I felt no wiser after reading it.

A bitter message to his adversary?
A trace of old city quarter rivalry?

Why in a line of common choices
was this sentence picked as "the one"
deserving its own exhibition
at Heworth Metro station?

And why this need to expose one's failure
on a two and a half metre high wall?

At the bottom of his blurred printed picture –
                          36 was his number –

I am not even the greatest
distance runner in Gateshead.

Kevin Cadwallender Introduces Adam Peardon

Kevin Cadwallender was born in 1958 in Hartlepool. He has been active on the north east poetry scene for ages. A former editor of *Hybrid* poetry magazine and press, he is co-ordinator of *Origins* poetry and music club. He was also the demo editor for Newcastle-based music magazine *Get Rhythm* from 1998-2002 and editor and founder of *Sand* magazine. His books and collections include Baz Uber Alles (Dog Eater, 2005), The Last Great Northern Whale (Rookbook, 1993) and Public (Iron Press, 2001) and about a dozen pamphlets by various publishers. Plays produced include The Man, which was commissioned for Peterlee Festival in 1987 and various children's productions.

'The mentoring process for me is less about correction of perceived faults or the imposition of my own poetic will and more about the preservation of the authentic voice. With this in mind the process was a barter with exchanges and acceptance of suggestions and ideas noted, taken and not taken and those suggestions sparking new ideas. My mentee's individual voice is preserved in all of its dynamism. Adam Peardon's poems reveal themselves slowly on the consciousness and spread outwards in ripples of understanding.'

Adam Peardon is currently at Leeds University reading Philosophy. He was a founder member of the Hydrogen Jukebox Cabaret Team, often appearing with the alternative music and spoken word combo Industrial Junkies with whom he also performed at the Durham Literature festival and The Verb Garden in Middlesbrough. As a performance poet he has done support slots with the likes of his mentor Kevin Cadwallender and Matt Caley and more recently has read at venues around Leeds.

Removed

When writing a poem about moving house,
One should not use bric a brac in anyway
And discard the use of 'discard' and try if you
Are at all able not to anthropomorphise your house.
Don't look back, it will look at you with sad square eyes
Even the removal men are
Having trouble lifting the sentiment
That is gathering in your head.

Having moved once, don't fall into the
Trap of writing about it a second time
The same old empty boxes and yes maybe
Even tea chests
(If you are moving in the Victorian era)
Will appear and you will be forced
To review your possessions
As if they are metaphorical,
They are not and stop thinking of similes for
Unseen clocks ticking in boxes!
Don't you dare use words like 'Flotsam'
Lock all doors, watch the walls sighing.

Don't even bother reaching for a pen,
When words like 'nostalgia and memorabilia'
Are near. Get a ladder,
Clear the bird's nest out of the guttering.
Avoid titles like 'Home from Home'
Anything but that or 'Once Removed'
The slow decline into pun,
(Heading off into the punset)
Thank God it is over
And brace yourself
For the next time.

Tell all your friends how stressful
It has all been, milk their sympathy,
Turn up your collar as you walk past
The man with a dog in the shop doorway,
The Big Issue seller that makes you deaf.
The money in your pocket safe as houses.

The King of Borneo

Hair matted, unkempt
Face unshaved, unwashed
Overcoat fights off the cold
Stiffening his bones.
Laugh at him,
Look down on him,
Mostly just avoid him
As he sits on his concrete throne,
You can give him money and food
But cannot find him his pride
Now he accepts his place.
Borneo a distant fantasy.

Bent Ego

He had good taste in clothes,
Sharply dressed from head to toe
A little make up and fine cologne
He radiated style.
I radiated B.O. and beer breath
And my jumper smelled faintly of
The chicken tandoor I'd eaten
The night before the night before last.
Unkempt hair, in need of a shave,
Clothes faded and stained and mismatched
I don't know how to dress
For Fuck's sake, I'm a mess!

But I can be witty, and burp on cue.
I do a great routine about how my cock's huge
And yours is so small it's been subsumed
But he; he could command the room
With a style and ease that made him seem
Quite pleasing to the fairer sex.
He had his choice of any one of
About nine or ten, but he preferred
The company of men, who would approach him
Again, and again and again.

But I; I sigh. Oh my *deary* me
I was propositioned by Beryl
A friend of the landlord's auntie-
Can't he call her off?
She's twice my age and size
Her thickset thighs testing
Her jeans at the seams,
A roll from her waist shines brightly white
As it peeks from beneath her over-tight blouse
What a sight! I'd prefer the company of men.
But still – as she whispered
Wicked words in my ear, I couldn't help
But draw her near
The attention was nice, and she tried to entice me
With a wink and a smile, she fondled my thigh
Oh why, would I entertain this?

Her diabetic blubber felt soft to touch
And as I reached between her many love-handles

The scandal excited, ignited my lust
I grabbed a hunk, between her hip and her bust
As we stumbled out back for a fumble,
Thoughts jumbled with a breathy passion
My heightened excitement exploded
Over her fleshy palm, hhhaaaaaah!
I exhaled deeply to calm myself down
And glanced around with renewed clarity
My prior sense of disparity returned
Like a brick through the window of my
Cloudy self-conscious.
Feeling suddenly sober, I declared the date over
And shuffled solemnly back to the bar.

As I mused that I needed a life,
He was having the time of his.
His sophisticated demeanor left people vying
To buy him a drink
He showed his gratitude with a smile and a wink
And I began to think how I wished I could be
Sharply dressed from head to toe
Maybe no makeup, but a splash of cologne
Then I too could radiate style.

Meanwhile, he had pulled
A Spanish exchange student named José.
I don't care if he was gay
That he slept with men
At the end of the day,
He was proud of the tanned man
Who linked his arm with sophisticated charm,
They left the bar with heads held high
And each with someone to love
Who would still be there the morning after,
Smiling.
All I was left with
Was a handful of dry roasted, piled
On a soggy beer mat, and *that*
Is my legacy.
The bar's now empty.
I gather my coat and brace myself
For the cold, wet,
Pathetic
Fallacy.

Kate Fox Introduces Rebecca Moran

Kate Fox was a radio journalist for several years and came to poetry via stand up comedy. She likes the sea, chocolate, diagnosing personality disorders and laughing. Her book of poems *Why I* was published by Zebra Publishing in 2005 and her pamphlet *We are not Stone* was published as part of Ek Zuban's Anglo-Finnish collaborations in 2007. She has won poetry slams across the country, received a Time to Write grant from the Arts Council in 2005 and was the 2006 recipient of New Writing North's Andrew Waterhouse Award.

'Reading Rebecca's courageous, strong poems was inspirational for me and it was exciting to be able to enter into a dialogue with her about ways to go further in creating the effects she was creating. Rebecca truly is uluwa- the cyclone "who leaves changes in her wake" and this mentoring was a two way process where mentor and mentee were changed, just as a good poem should change both poet and reader.'

Rebecca Moran was born on a cattle farm in rural Western Australia in 1982. She has recently studied creative writing modules at The University of Teesside and performed her songs at many North East venues, including The Morden Tower.

"I've been in love with words since I first learnt the alphabet. As a child I spent many hours in the glorious universe of books, and many more hanging upside down from trees and swings, composing songs and dreaming that our school music teacher would come to buy cows, hear me sing, and apologise for not letting me join the choir. I hitchhiked around my fantastic country as a barefoot gypsy teenager, learning to play guitar and building a reputation as a songwriter. Always, I carried a notebook and have saved my own life many times by writing what I could not bear to feel. Working with Kate has done me boundless good as an artist and writer. She has given me previously unfelt confidence in my work, and in the importance of it. I was stunned when editing my work with Kate that she got not just a vague impression of my point from my words, but managed to go beyond understanding them as I hoped and show me things I had not seen myself. Equally important Kate has taught me to edit, edit, edit!"

From the Fred and Rose poems

19.

He is the uncredited director.
Playing, pausing, fastforwarding,
rewinding, splicing, cutting.
She is the star
in the re-enactment
of his worst fears.
Their tapes and videos
will not corrupt like memory.
He can lose her again and again,
she is still there.
He loses himself again and again,
he is still there.
No matter how close in
they zoom,
they will never find
what isn't there.
Someone can see you
you must be there.
Someone can hear you
you must be there.
Someone can feel you
you must be there
you must be there.

Psychopaths (Are Not Nice People)

Your laughing eyes as you dare me to fight
And then use my own weapon against me
You laughed. Laughed. Laughed.

Sharp steel, soft flesh are married
And oh, the sickly sound a stabbing makes

Most people do not know this.

Psychopaths are not nice people
And I still smell blood. Everywhere. I. Go.

Jekyll and Hyde, Hyde and Jekyll
You raped me, then you bathed me

Clever bastard, aren't ya

Parkinsonian tremors, my own thousand yard stare

Blood smells like wet rust.

Uluwa

I never knew I could fly
Till that storm kissed me
Lightning gave me wings
Burnt my feet and hurt like hell though
I only flew two metres

97 Mosquito bites'll drive you crazy
If you got no tee-tree to soothe em
And them fire ants,
They'll make you think you're dyin
Even the plants are vicious;
Razor grass, a paper cut between your toes

Cyclone comin; no time for a girl on her own in the bush
Drive 6 hours up a road that's flowing the other way
Pindan dirt stains me red

I love this land.

Bardi tribe teach me to fish
Eat dugong and sea turtle
Make spears, find good bush tucker

Name me Uluwa- the cyclone that blows from place to place
Leaving changes in its wake

I play them my music
Teach art to the kids
Draw their portraits in place of school photos

This is no-mans land
This is my land

Paul Summers Introduces Michael Edwards

Paul Summers was born in Blyth, Northumberland in 1967. He was founding co-editor of the 'Leftfield' magazines *Billy Liar* and *Liar Republic* and has been responsible for facilitating countless creative projects across the North in educational and community contexts. He has performed his work all over the world.

Home (in 3 bits), a spoken word/music collaboration with Dave Hull-Denholm was launched in 2006 as was his latest collection, *'big bella's dirty cafe'* (dogeater books).

Other publications include: *Cunawabi* (Cunawabi Press 2003), *The Rat's Mirror* (Lapwing Press 1999), *The Last Bus* (Iron Press 1998), *Beer & Skittles* (Echo Room Press 1997), *Vermeer's Dark Parlour* (Echo Room Press 1996), *140195* (Echo Room Press 1995)

"I've always liked Mike's work; he's very interesting as a writer of prose but equally interesting as a poet. He's clever, he's funny, confident in his voice and he's got a good ear/eye for spotting the epiphanous or the darkly comedic in the mundane. He's an exciting prospect, one to keep an eye on. The two pieces we worked on hopefully demonstrates all of the above."

Michael Edwards recently completed a degree in English and Media Studies at the University of Teesside and is now studying for an MA in Creative Writing at Northumbria University. He has had work published in *KENAZ*, *Fresh* (Ek Zuban 2006), and *Discoverers* (Mudfog 2005). He is currently working on a novel and a collection of short stories.

'I'd meet Paul at The Bridge pub in Newcastle and we'd plough through poems and half-poems and non-poems and any other scribbling I'd brought along. I was hoping Paul might want to work on the 'Parcel' poem but I was surprised he picked the 'Sympathy' one. It was originally a tiny thing but Paul seemed to like its 'spine'. He encouraged me to fatten it right up and then, once it was suitably bloated, together we hacked away at it. Now it's the 'Sympathy' poem that, for me, best sums up the mentorship. You can see Paul's influence in it but it is still 'me'. One of my most abiding memories of the mentorship is looking at a draft of the 'Sympathy' poem and asking Paul in all earnestness: What word do you think best describes the arse of a stone tortoise?'

Broken Land
(delhi surface mine, blagdon, northumberland.)

arnie stuffs the remnants of an over-ripe
banana into his gob. *"how'd you know
that's a fitters' car?"* rhetorical question.

*"it's had a fucking flat tyre for ten weeks
& he still hasn't got 'round to putting
the cunt right!"* everyone laughs

apart from stobbart. the *cb* crackles
in a distant storm: the air-con is buggered
on the *triple 7*, cooking dougie's feet

like a sunday roast. at *cut 10*
they're down onto coal. the *dh120*
crawls over to help, stripping

the last two foot of fireclay &
white thill, exposing as it does, the
glint of the *high main's* perfect jet

& brenkley's legacy of linear cuts,
a weave of neat roads, their roofs
collapsed, each groaning strata

subsided, their rolleyways rusted now,
twisted & arthritic, & caught like fossils
in the cold grip of grey shale, a line of

extant tubs, their buckled sides
sucked in like a chain-smoker's
cheeks. deserted & abandoned,

driven out by wet, or worse,
or curse; the past revealing
its faults. & over bait

a litany of *easyjet* jaunts, of
gob-shite wisdom, the patterns
of their frozen words lost

in the fog of steaming tea.
& there's a deer by the lagoons,
proud & still, a statue captured

in the turquoise sheen,
the crackle glaze of reeds
reflected, drawing cross-hairs

on its perfect flank. & two young
hares play *chasey* on the overburden
mound, their fur burnished copper,

every muscle taut as a bow-string.
a thin seam of cloud shimmers
in pale skies & ian's calm eyes

mirrored in the steel of the auger
bit. high on the re-shaped bund
damp earth slumps, a river

of boulder clay tumbling
down the steps & outside
the fitter's cabin, three

generations of feral cats
bask in rare october sun.
the one minute siren squeals

its warning, blunt echoes
ricocheting off the southern wall;
the plant silenced, a neat rank

of bore-holes readying themselves
for the hit. it comes like lightning
over sea. the thud of the *det*

discharged, the ripple of displaced
stone, a shock-wave rising, climbing
your legs like autumn damp.

a brief dance of orange smoke
hanging like genies over the shelf
& the dust will settle, as usual,

the calloused earth split,
the vacuum sigh of separation,
the slow lurch of broken land.

Waiting in for a parcel

The television gurns a litany of
Garden-decking and French property,
Outside: wheeled-bins, domino-lined,
A postman groping house to house.
I contemplate a wank.

Resigned gents checking tyres,
Brillo-headed ladies
Easing tartan-trolleys
Over calloused potholes.
Next door: the tune from *Neighbours* plays.

A voice resembling a whistling kettle,
Screams playtime-orders from the fields,
A man shoos leaves from a dank drive,
Cups a cigarette, exhaling a sigh of smoke.
I decide to watch the end of *Doctors*.

Later on the mat,
A slip of paper:
Sorry we missed you.
Will call again later.

Mispelt Sympathy

A pot-bellied kid
Loads his *Supersoaker*
Launches a volley
At gaping sunroofs

Sammy sniffs the grilled-air
Butts his nose against
The frigid arse
Of a stone tortoise

I pull him up sharp
At a lamppost stump
A badly bandaged thumb
Amongst sunburnt bungalows

I recall *The Evening Gazette*
A stamp-sized story
Beneath the results
Of the midweek lottery

A report concerning a lad
Some lasses, a party
A wobbled-croggie
On a borrowed moped

And my Dad a Quincy fan
Astutely diagnosing
He'll have been drinking
Maybe's even drugs?

On a slumped wreath
There's a card that reads:
Now you sleep with the angles

Cynthia Fuller Introduces Laura Severi

Cynthia Fuller was born in Kent in 1948. She has lived in County Durham since 1979. She works freelance in adult and higher education, teaching literature and creative writing, and runs writing workshops with groups in the community. She worked as a poetry editor for the magazine *Writing Women* for 12 years, and more recently co-edited *Smelter* (Mudfog Press, 2003) with Kevin Cadwallender, *The Poetry Cure* (Bloodaxe, 2005) with Julia Darling, and *North by North-East* (Iron Press, 2006) with Andy Croft. She has had four books of poems published by Flambard Press – *Moving Towards Light* (1992); *Instructions for the Desert* (1996); *Only a Small Boat* (2001) and *Jack's Letters Home* (2006).

'Mentoring provides a great opportunity to work closely with a poet and to really explore the poetry in depth. It's different from teaching because it's more informal and allows time for more attention to be given to the work. With this project I found the idea of 'the wilds' immediately inspiring and a poem was taking shape before I read Laura's work. Then I read Laura's poems and one particularly –'Clipped' – chimed with the mood of what I'd started. Her imagery was really strong and startling. My poem sharpened its focus and narrative and I was able to finish it. I can't explain the 'dialogue' between the poems, but know it was there."

Laura Severi is 20, she comes from Darlington. She has just finished studying an access course at Newcastle College. She is also a singer/songwriter with a 'Riot Girrl' stance, a web and games designer and has been a regular performer at The Hydrogen Jukebox, KENAZ LIVE and other events across the region. Her poems have been published in *KENAZ* magazine and on various websites.

'Before the mentoring experience of 'The Wilds' my writing was completely personalised, in the way that the subject, in the core of every poem was my self. Working with Cynthia, made me think outside the lines of my usual creative sphere.'

Sanctuary

Dumped at the roadside, all her thoughts broken,
mouth no longer her mouth, see her dart
like a creature freed from the headlamps
into the forest's safe dark.

Bare feet are not hurt by the carpet
of pine needles. Moss staunches bleeding.
Moonlight cools bruises. Her blood beat
will settle now, her body cease shaking.

Her heart as it calms knows no harm is meant
in the scuffle of paws, no danger
for her in the rustle of dead leaves.
She is no prey for wild hunters.

She lets low branches whip back, relishes
sharp thorns and nettles, clean pain to wipe out
the marks of soiled fingers, cold earth to
put out her belly's hurt burning.

Her pulse slows, around her a new rhythm,
tuned to the owl's wing brushing the darkness,
the flare of the fox as he catches a scent,
the delicate hesitancy of the deer.

And perhaps she will stay, let the wildness take her,
her scraped arms resting, eyelids closing,
tangled hair a nest for earwigs and woodlice,
bruised mouth a fruit on the forest floor.

Clipped

Dead spiders limp from my lids
Flake upon my cheek
Air suck in, out, through crimson threads

So much black in between

Gut spews its bile upon my tongue
A ragweed knot of veins and shit

As he showers I lay like a rag doll
Or a pin cushion
I finger the berry mucus

So much black in between

His form drawn into every sofa
Fisting my hair
I on my knees

So much black in between

The Boy with No Shadow

Benjamin traced his veins
His fingers like roots crept up
The pulsating green

The womb is barren
Catholic bind severed
Rotten seed, they hissed

His fingers like roots crept up
Over the white image of his childhood
Never to be seen

Clutching the gate of hell
Her outline would crack against his skull
Rotten seed, they hissed

The sly murmurs of nuns would pierce the lull
Closed head hung like a sour cat
Rotten seed, she hissed
Never to be seen

Ghazala Bashir Introduces Khadim Hussain

Ghazala Bashir was born in Middlesbrough and held the title of Middlesbrough's Poet Laureate in 1999. She had a pamphlet of poems published by Mudfog Press in the same year entitled *No Small Fire*. She has read at live literature events in the North and participated in the Ek Zuban translation and cross cultural workshops. She had a joint collection with the Finnish poet Henry Lehtonen *The Wall Between Us* published by Ek Zuban in July 2007. In 2000 she left Middlesbrough to travel around Europe. She is currently living in France and teaches English as a second language.

Khadim Hussain is 49 years old and lives in Middlesbrough. Worked as an Experimental Assistant in the Research and Development Department of I.C.I, Wilton and has recently written a book *Going for a Curry? A Social and Culinary History* which documents the settlement, development and impact of the 'Indian' population in Middlesbrough. He took Creative Writing Courses at the University of Teesside and with the efforts of the tutors, Bob Beagrie and Andy Willoughby, was able to develop the book from a dry history topic to a broader appeal. Since attending the writing course he has started writing plays and poetry.

"The mentoring programme was very useful because for the first time someone looked at my poetry with a critical eye. Ghazala felt the poem 'Bury Me' was not finished and should be expanded and 'transport the reader to that place'. Through our exchange I've learnt to be more critical of my work and review it from the readers' point of view."

Scorpion

Once upon a time
In a quiet terraced street
young Zeesha, consumed with rage
Came tumbling down the stairs
With her hair on fire.

Her scorpion tail which used to swing,
High and low, stung her temper
Because Zeesha had no power
Over her hair.

These days Zeesha sports a cropped look
Feels empowered being accepted
By those who only respected long tails.

Her younger sisters,
Swing their highlighted and straightened
Layered and toned,
Bollywood style manes
Which they've chosen to grow

In the hope of blinding
men and women alike
With jealousy.

Bury Me

Bury me not in a cemetery
Don't cover my grave
With gravel and cement.

Sacrifice no flowers,
Upon my grave
Leave nature's bounty to nature.

Bury me near a river glade
Where the water buffalos graze
And roam over me.

When the river is full
And floods the glade
I'll be thankful
For the bathing.

Please bury me, bury me
In the river glade
Where as a child
I once played.

If Only...

Get up!
You'll be late for school!
Did you wash your face?
Behind the ears too?
Clean your teeth and use fresh miswak
Comb your hair!
Hurry up, eat your breakfast
and change your clothes!
Walk on the path to school
Not through the fields!

If only...
I was a maali,
Weeding and watering the plants,
Waking up at my leisure
Eating breakfast at my pace
Not bothering to change my night clothing.

My salwar and kameez
Soiled with dust
From weeding and digging
And walking through fields of crops,
The signs of my industry.

If only...
I was a charwan
Tending the maijah by the river glades.
I'd lean against a tree or lay on the lush grass
In its shade and play my flute
To my heart's content.
I'd carry my lathi over my shoulder
Like Maula Jatt's gandasa
Strut across my domain,
Return to the village at milking time.

Miswak: a softened stick used as a toothbrush, **Maali:** gardener, **Salwar and Kameez:**
traditional Indian clothes, **Charwan:** herdsman, **Majjah:** female buffalo, **Lathi:** staff,
Maula Jatt: the hero of Punjabi film, tougher than Rambo, **Gandasa:** an axe like blade

Bob Beagrie Introduces Katie Metcalfe

Bob Beagrie was born in Middlesbrough. He has worked as a literature development worker and creative writing tutor and is currently self employed as a freelance writer on a wide range of educational and social projects and residencies. He is co-editor of *KENAZ* magazine and co-runs Writing Visions Cabaret in Middlesbrough. Publications include, *Gothic Horror* (Mudfog 1997), *Masque: The Art of the Vampire* (Mudfog 2000), *Huggin & Munnin* (Biscuit 2002), *Endeavour: Newfound Notes* (Biscuit 2004), *Perkele* (Ek Zuban 2006), and a forthcoming collection *Yoik* (Cinnamon Press 2008). He is currently writing a verse novel about Mother Shipton called The Dropping Well. His poems have appeared in various anthologies and magazines and he has performed across the U.K. and Europe. He has recently been poet in residence at The Dylan Thomas Centre, Swansea.

'Katie is a determined young writer who has managed to turn her early experiences of self harm and isolation into a deep seated motivation for writing. She has said that "writing saved her life", and the commitment she gives to her work reflects this. It has been a pleasure to see her work evolve during the mentoring sessions, to see how she is experimenting with style, voice and writing through different masks. Her work attempts to tease out some of the wild drives that lie just beneath the surface of the civilized suburban lifestyle.'

Katie Metcalfe is 20, a published author and poet. Between 14-18 she suffered with anorexia. She began writing her first book *Sticks and Stones*, while in hospital at the age of 15, which she self-published. Her most recent book *Anorexia: A Stranger in the Family* is published by Accent Press and has been featured in local and national press and media. She regularly performs at writing events in Teesside, and had articles and poetry published in *KENAZ* and various anthologies. Currently, she has two novels in progress and an abundance of poetry underway.

'Confidence within every aspect of my writing and poetry performance has increased beyond belief.'

The City With The Beautiful Far Away Mind

I climb the old wooden roller coaster
on Linnanmaki.
                    Cool wind,
                              clear night.
A few hours before the dawn even the harbour
                    is asleep,
though Suomelina's ever watchful
of the sea and the land,
                         the White Palace is snoring
as I edge along a joist and squeeze quietly
                                   onto the tracks.
Inertia binds this fun park.
          The stalls, the bars, the booths
                    are padlocked and shuttered.
The Waltzers and T-pots are dreaming,
          The Big Wheel cradles its cages.
The Hall of Mirrors is locked up like a multiform freak
          to gaze endlessly into itself.
                              No security
nor guard dogs nor cctv, so I walk the steep slope
          of the first big drop,
                         imagining thousands of screams
falling like dead leaves tumbling down the rocks
to the city below,
becoming snagged in the fence
          or the tangle of bushes,
                    stepped on,
                         rained on
and buried by the first snows of the season.

The city is lit up now,
                    twinkling, its limits
defined by black forest, black sea.
          The drinkers and dancers have spilled,
sweaty,
from the night clubs,
          eaten at a grilli and ambled
homeward to peel off their layers
and fall
          into fucking then sleeping.

Somewhere
        down there Satu feels a kick,
                        wakes with a craving
for a reindeer steak, her child swims,
                turns and makes her breasts ache.
The semi-pro wrestler
who wants to defend his nation
                from immigrants,
        and played his air guitar
on stage in The Rock
            to Bohemian Rhapsody
now sits in a chair splashed by lamplight
suppressing
        homo-erotic impulses by leafing
            through a porn mag before hitting the sack.
The retired history teacher
        with his home counties accent,
who bought me a Salmiakki in the karaoke bar,
            collapses drunk on his single bed.
He will dream sporadically
            until eight
of Andy Cap fighting in the Winter War with Flo.
In the cobbled square
        two policemen are trying to flush
a human spider
        out of the bus shelter and into their van.
He has taken to moving on all fours,
                arched in a crab
his eyes wild through the strands of his long lank hair,
while his mouth is moving,
            chewing,
only a wordless
        mewling emerges.
He has lost all of his words
            with his bus fare down the drain,
where they echo to him through the dripping sewers.

On the top
        of the roller coaster
I smoke a cigarette, then sit very still,
watching for the advance of winter,
        wondering

                    if I'll remember the way back
to the apartment,
            feeling the pulse of the slumbering,
                    restless city
through the planks of old timber.
I suspect
        I could fly
but know its a long way down to the ground from here,
                the drops are steep,
I'll need to step with care and realise
            with a shiver
                it's high time I submitted to gravity,
let the night and all of its lightness pass,
                                    time

to pull myself together and find a bed
to fall into.

Missing My Ribcage

I miss my ribcage from time to time
And the comforting, velvety downy hair
I sometimes hope that when I awake
[1] Ana will be there.
I miss the kick
Of watching my skin spilt.
The old me
The one never ignored.
The streets would always whisper
And the walls would always talk.
I was the ethereal, the different
The one walking a thin silver thread.
Would she make it, wouldn't she?
I was the unusual, the mystery.
Those news reports of starvation,
Sometimes I wish they were me.

[1] Anorexia is growing into a religion on the internet,
where the followers worship their goddess 'Ana',
short for Anorexia Nervosa.

Diluted

Crunched cans, stubbed fag butts
Syringes and filth,
Pizza and stains of mouldy milk
Decorate the carpet.
I train eyes on him
Snorting the white stuff
Off a flattened porn mag
With pages stuck together.
Bitterness bubbles in my stomach
Scorching my insides
Disintegrating my affection.
Screaming 'Fuck off I hate you!'
I plough through the scum
Heading out for good, again,
As the drug invades his system.
The concrete courtyard greets me
Four intrusive towers loom,
Disorientation floods
As I collide with the slick, murky mire.
My head hits a gum tattooed pavement
And I relive the ordeal again,
So I pray to our Lord Jesus,
John Lennon, Uncle Bob's son.
This isn't the relationship I'd planned.
Nor the love I'd had in mind.
He'll wander down in a minute, I'm sure
Find me crushed in the cracks of the street
He'll ask for sex when he picks me up
And stare with those diluted eyes.
I'll agree of course, like I always have
And he'll drag me home satisfied.

Angela Readman Introduces Jennifer Peardon

Angela Readman comes from Middlesbrough and lives in Newcastle. She won the Biscuit poetry competition in 2004, followed by the publication of her collection *Sex with Elvis*. She has had work published by Iron Press, Diamond Twig, and with the Finnish poet Tapani Kinnunen in *Hardcore* (Ek Zuban, 2006). She has had work specially commissioned by The Hydrogen Jukebox and was part of The Flesh of The Bear exchange between North Eastern and Finnish poets. She is currently working on a collection, *Strip*, to be published by Salt.

'The most satisfying part of being a writer is when the opportunity arises to encourage. It was really exciting to work with Jenny and see the poems evolve. I don't really like the word mentor, all I hoped to do was help someone look again. Sometimes it is as simple as pointing out what the strengths are in the work, because as writers, the lack of faith to complete things can be our biggest hurdle. We are all striving to be better all the time, if we aren't we shouldn't write. The joy in this process was being reminded, seeing a lack of complacency, later looking at my own work with new eyes.'

Jennifer Peardon was born in Scotland in 1982 she describes her life –

"I travelled a lot during my childhood: from Kent to Malaysia and from Indonesia to…well erm…Darlington! I started writing and performing poetry and music as a founder member of The Hydrogen Jukebox Cabaret of the Spoken Word. I am now living happily with my partner and two children in Newcastle and studying English language at Newcastle University. It's great, life's great and I'm very happy – but don't worry I never let that get in the way of a good poem! My mentor for this project was Angela Readman, it has been an enlightening experience working with her and her attention to detail is second to none. She helped me to lose my '-ing's and helped my flailing punctuation along enormously. I really feel I benefited from the process!"

The Trade

It's all part of the business.
The building on stilts down the lane,
and a tin roof making tuning forks from the thaw.

When she was small they held her hand all the way,
let a small fox wrap her hand in the pockets of ears.
She looks at foxes, foxes look back.
She is not sure if they are dog or cat,
thinks they are not sure if she is people or pup.
She points to a door leading further back.
The breeze mumbles as she's led away.

Later it will show itself to her.
She will wander through pens of pups
and edge open the door to a room
where father is big, a blur of lumberjack.
The same motion that splinters the logs
tosses heads on a pile with useful hands.

Same heavy hands hoist her on his shoulders,
thick fingers wrapping round ankles,
firm and safe as a clamp.

The light brights everything white.
Father blurred into angel, double exposed,
motion lines and the ghost of him overlap
with the man tacking pelts onto a frame
till they fail to turn away.
Skin curling at the edges
the way leaves find their solace
before they give in to weather,
like the last leaf on the apple tree one winter,
she pressed between the pages of a bible,
dreamt of, but never looked at again.

When he sees her his mouth uncoils
from a scar to a smile,
as hands wipe themselves
and he lifts her into the drying closet,
to fold her hand in soft silver fur.

'Soft, huh?' She nods.

This is what snow should feel like
when it wraps up the house
and makes everything quiet.
His arms radiate heat as she rubs a collar
and he tells her' Feel. All these
will adorn a beautiful woman someday.'

It's a life she is born to learn,
how to feed a runt one tear of milk at a time,
select the bitch that yields the most young.
Better here than in China.

She is learning the trade,
making sure there's no waste,
except heads she wants to learn
to say all look the same,
but each fox seems to have its own face.

Expressions piled like windfall,
the heavy certain sound of the toss,
of one onto another, in various stages of yawn
half smiles, some laughing,
some unamazed by the in-joke.

Outside snow blows out footprints
as soon as they are made towards home.
Father walks all the way sideways
so she stays dry, half white, half dark,
as they cross into the porch.
The fire roars greeting as they enter inside.
Father takes off his coat.
Brother eats.
Mother talks.
Snow drifts.
One day all this will be hers.

Snap Shots of Malaysia

Shanty town by a river the colour of mocha,
corrugated iron roofs, and cardboard looking walls.
Children play in ragged shorts, laughing
with bright eyes and no futures.

The twin towers, symmetrical and imposing
dominate the cityscape
like two dauntingly majestic kings
permanently locked in check mate.

Our house; big and white - almost stately.
Me and mum in the pool, drinking bucks fizz
Dad on the porch with a cigar -
in his 'lord of the manor' pose.

Palm trees and orchids,
tropical and beautiful, but never changing.
Me in the foreground, donning a head scarf
trying the culture for size.

Sharpe Street

I am drifting through changing climates,
monsoon dreams of my childhood
and regional accents, I don't regret it
but I sometimes feel stranded
and I get itchy feet.

I went to Strathclyde Park for a "shot on the shoot"
aged 5, with almost blonde hair
and what my Mum called chameleon eyes.
I remember the slide,
wanting to go down it backwards
and not quite being brave enough.

I remember having friends round to play
in the sandpit my dad made out of bricks
left over from the garage
- I don't remember the garage.

Walking round the loch,
throwing stones at the water
I tried to make them skip
satisfied with a splash, and not feeling the cold.
Now when my own children shrug their coats off in winter I say:
"You don't feel it at that age, I remember."

Mostly I remember the prompts – stories and photos
super-imposed over my own flickering recollections.
The thing I remember best is leaving;
the cat jumping on Dad's head in the car,
the long drive and the excitement.
I wasn't sad.
I didn't know what it meant.

Keith Armstrong Introduces P.A. Morbid

Keith Armstrong was born in Heaton, Newcastle upon Tyne, where he has worked as a community development worker, poet, librarian and publisher. Now residing in Whitley Bay he is coordinator of the Northern Voices creative writing and community publishing project which specialises in recording the experiences of people in the North East of England.

He has been a self-employed writer since 1986 and was recently awarded a PhD on the work of Newcastle writer Jack Common at the University of Durham. He was Year of the Artist 2000 poet-in-residence at Hexham Races. His poetry has been extensively published in magazines such as *New Statesman*, *Poetry Review*, *Dream Catcher* & *Other Poetry* as well as in the collections *The Jingling Geordie, Dreaming North, Pains of Class* and *Imagined Corners* (Smokestack), on cassette, LP & CD, and on radio & TV.

'Morbid's poetry is steeped in the North Sea and the landscape of Cleveland. It connects the inner soul with a certain bleakness and poignancy. As an old sea dog myself who suffers frequent pangs of North East melancholy, I identify strongly with Morbid's writing and was pleased to have the opportunity to act as a mentor. Mostly, we conducted our dialogue via email and phone but, as you might expect, we also shared a few bottles of brown face to face! I didn't want to alter the mood of the poems, only to offer my experience in shaping them. I think it worked.'

P.A. Morbid has been writing for a number of years now, his main themes being Memory and Loss. The Memory of Loss and the Loss of Memory. He laughs sometimes, but not overmuch. Insomnia and Unrequited Love are his bedfellows. He also paints and makes music, mostly unlistenable.

'Working with Keith Armstrong helped me polish up my work, removing a verse and adding a question mark and a title in questionable taste. Happy days Keith, thank you!'

In The Spanking Roger

This must be
the lowest hour
of the low.
I am
wet through in the dog-end gutter
of a whiplashed Manchester,
where the rain
bolts down
and the darkness
simply soaks you
to the guts of your soul.
I am
a lost boy,
drenched
from the black Pennines;
a stranger drinking
a glass of gloom
with Thatcher's underclass.
Here, in the Spanking Roger,
Miles Platting,
they are all
making a racket,
working the rotting
system.
You can get
touched up
for a tanner
or spanked,
wanked
and rogered
for a bob.
It's all in a sodden carrier bag,
a greasy spoon;
all in
a backstreet cruise,
a sopping blow job,
a blob
for a raindrop:
this Manchester-wet
dream.

The Poet, 1986...

The horizon seems to go on forever, in a line of dove grey cloud above, ash grey water below. While at my feet the water laps the damp sand, shale grey and dark, dark as my eye follows it out. To the bigger waves. White-topped, freezing. Walking along the beach to Marske I wonder. Where has this heaviness come from? That I can't just wish it away. The wind dying down, even as the rain starts pelting my face. Where does this pressure come from, that I can walk like this and wish there were some painless way of not being? Huddled into my overcoat, the mist closing in around me as I plod on. Along the beach to Marske. Getting closer and closer to the disappointment I know I'm going to find there.

12:31 am. Thursday 5th of October 2006

A slight case of overdosing

What was I thinking?
I know I didn't want to die.

Not really.

I just wanted all the hurting to stop.
To find some release from wanting
to be drunk constantly.

I didn't want to leave this world behind,
my son without a father. Parents without a son.

Leaving a hole in their lives and achieving nothing.
But more pain, more hurt.

So here I am
hooked up to a glucose drip

watching the rain spit against the window
and fade in the long hours of boredom

watching the glucose drip
drip, drip

I'm lost, I see that now.
More clearly than I've ever seen it.
Since the last time anyway.

I'm lost because it's easier to be lost
than struggle and fail to find my way.

The spectre of victory is enough to drag me on.
On and on and over the same old ground.

Barely moving.

At home in this despair, this lack of movement.
Turning underachieving into an art.
The art of putting life off.

Andy Willoughby Introduces Julie Egdell

Andy Willoughby is a poet, educational playwright and drama director from Middlesbrough. He was co-founder of The Hydrogen Jukebox Cabaret of the Spoken Word in Darlington and is co-editor of *KENAZ* magazine. He has published two collections, *The Wrong California* (Mudfog 2004) and *Tough* (Smokestack Books 2005), a collaborative pamphlet with Finnish poet and novelist Riina Katajavuori, *Peripheries* (Ek Zuban 2006) and appears in various anthologies. He performs his work regularly, often with musicians, nationally and internationally.

'It has been a very rewarding process working with Julie over a period of time. I concentrated on helping her develop her own voice and seek material from her own experience. I have seen her work move from being heavily influenced by nineteenth century literature to becoming more vitally concerned with the contemporary world. In her initial work I liked the way she engaged with myth and dreamscapes, primarily inspired by her reading of Tennyson and Blake, I didn't want her to lose the sense of epiphany and visionary moments so we concentrated on the wilds in journeys and altered states. My own poem, Liquorice Fish developed out of this process as we discussed the use and creation of new myths to deal with the modern world.'

Julie Egdell is 21 and originally from Whitley Bay near Newcastle, but moved to Middlesbrough to study English at the University of Teeside. Since moving two years ago she has had the time of her life, both creatively and personally. She has published poems in *KENAZ* magazine and performed at Writing Visions Cabaret and at KENAZ LIVE. She recently won an award from The Teesside University Student Union for her campaigning journalism.

'Since starting the mentoring sessions I have started writing all the time, about ordinary things in my day to day life. I have gained a lot more confidence in my own writing and have been introduced to the work of contemporary writers I can really relate to such as Charles Bukowksi and Sharon Olds. Andy has shown me different techniques and exercises that can get the most out of my writing. He also helped me to discover the writing culture in Middlesbrough which is so alive and exciting.'

Beware the Liquorice Fish of Helsinki!

They swim through the air late at night.
In the midsummer never-quite-dark
they play tricks on the body and mind

with graceful evasive manoeuvres,
they tickle the brain with quick tails
so 3am feels like the reveller's dusk.

You can only see them briefly -
Catch them with fly-quick eyes
Through the bottom of Salmiakki tumblers.

They will escape by tricking you
through your pleasure centres;
taunting you with unsated desire.

Your tongue may just lick their bellies
as they dive for the nightclub shadows
and all the drinks in gleaming bottles

promise that extra fix of sweetness
that will allow you one more dance -
a last chance to catch the ghost

of a good time, that departed
at midnight with Cinderella
in a tram full of Russian sailors.

Finally at sunrise they will lead you
to your suddenly spinning futon,
where you can catch one and devour it,

so you will awake with black lips
and a fish tail slamming back and forth
in your coffee desperate skull,

and you will look in vain under pillows
for that poem to end all poetry
promised you in sweet scaly whispers:

a line that would spawn a thousand lines,
weaving a net to hold the uneasy dreams
of all the city souls longing for some peace.

Glam Rock

My eyes scan the horizon
of the busy holiday town.
The dry, grey mountains
are obscured by white marble hotels.

There is an unnameable loneliness here –
though the gentle breeze soothes
the sun lovers on blue loungers
waiting for the clouds to melt away.

Your voice reads to me distantly.
A cockroach scurries out of the drain.
I am watching the family
by the cold pool below.

A Russian girl in a cowboy hat
and glam-rock sunglasses
orders another vodka and coke
from the poolside bar.

I imagine a hundred frightened voices
telling me their woes.
Here between the ocean and the mountains
lies a whole world of troubles.
I try to think of others but my own.

Landed

Nicotine intake breaks
I already distress.
In out, in out -
sharply a gasp for air.

The lights invade the dark,
flashing blue and green,
as I struggle to breathe –
a familiar scene.

The music here is bad,
the band cant get a break –
but no-one seems to care,
everyone's happy here.

At the bar I take a shot,
it burns. I chill it with
a swim in my cold glass
of bubbles and vodka.

I stumble to the loo's,
to pen some drunken words.
In the next stall I hear
Sobbing, sobbing.

Has she broken a nail?
"Earned" another slap?
Does her mortal state
realise love is unreturned?
Now she can't go back.

I head to the mirror,
douse myself in cheap perfume
and a lipstick called 'goddess'.
Pale face, eyes black
a cold, hard image stares back.

Maureen Almond Introduces Pamela Golden

Maureen Almond has lived in Teesside since she was two and was brought up 'below the railway' in Thornaby. She is currently undertaking a PhD at the University of Newcastle, pursuing her interest in the Roman poet, Horace and working on her fifth full collection of poetry. Her last collection, *The Works* is included in the Primary Texts Reading List for Oxford University Course, 'The Reception of Classical Literature in Twentieth-Century Poetry in English' and has recently been cited in the 'Cambridge Companion to Horace'.

'I thoroughly enjoyed mentoring for this project. I think one of the great things about this sort of activity, apart from meeting new people with whom you share an interest, is the opportunity it presents for the mentor to go on learning. It is a good feeling too, when you can help and encourage other people towards a love of poetry. It encourages us all when we see new people wanting to engage with it and coming to realise what a fantastic medium it is.'

Pamela Golden is a single parent and a mature student at Teesside University currently studying for an English and Media degree. She has taken extra courses in Creative Writing and Research and attended many workshops for poetry. She is the founder and chair of the student Union's Live Literature Society and has performed at KENAZ LIVE, Writing Visions and The Hydrogen Jukebox and has been published in *KENAZ* magazine. Having lived in Middlesbrough all her life she often walks on the Eston Hills and the beach at Redcar with her dog.

'I was thrilled to be chosen to be in this anthology. The help and advice I have received through mentoring has given me greater confidence in my work and helped me to look at my poems with a critical eye, re-read, re-edit before submitting it for publication. I found the advice and devices given have also created ideas for further poems. I shall look forward to any more mentoring schemes that will be offered.'

The Wild Train from Thornaby to Tyneside

fucks its way through a town of mis-matches,
picks up *we're-just-as-good-as-them* hoodies
i-pods the rest of us like we're nobodies,
makes us re-check pocket, bag, purse catches.

At Billingham the beanies come on board
paint scenes so vivid that by Hartlepool,
we know about last night, and with which fool
the little, spotty, skinny pricks have scored.

Seaham sees black-suited, stick-thin women
with cricket-sounding mobiles at their heads.
Sunderland's cosmopolitan and common
seem to tumble on the train straight from their beds.
People read through Heworth's empty station.
This must be what it feels like when you're dead!

Just Walking the Dog

The place is dark, desolate, deserted.
A biting wind whips and whistles;
branches reach out,
to tear the jacket from me.
Gravestones glisten like eerie phantoms;
disappear through swirls of fog,
disapprove of dogs' cocked legs
and the piss left on their cornerstones.

Distant tyres shush on tarmac
Orange furnace glow silhouettes nearby houses.
Crisp leaves catch in my hair
like bats looking for a place to hang.
My teeth chatter, breath escapes,
There's a smell of fresh earth.

The feathered grave of Moses,
surrounded by bags of potpourri
has a new structure of sticks and string;
a wigwam of respect
to the Canadian Mohawk Indian.*

Broken bottles dropped by a passing drunk
litter the frosty paths,
wait to catch unsuspecting paws.
Spider's webs caught on the hedgerow
are drenched in early morning dew.

Mud sucks and tugs at my feet
as if to pull me into an early grave.
Frightened rabbits scuttle
Squirrels squabble
Crows swoop overhead,
Caw-caw to a lone walker.

Squelching through the undergrowth
I cock my head.
Morning, I say, *Just walking the dog.*

* Refers to the grave of Moses Carpentor (Skrunyate), a Mohawk Indian buried in
Linthorpe Cemetary, Middlesbrough

Concrete Jungle

She walks the back streets and alleyways
Glances into passing cars
ready to hire out mouth, tits and arse.

Black roots show through dyed blond hair.
A painted face, circled by too many lines,
is pierced by large eyes that have seen too much.

She watches as they pick up younger models,
thinks of her kids; new shoes; designer gear;
spreads her legs for a fiver. Saves her kisses for him.

Nine till five, from hand to mouth
I seek relief from a day's work done.
Hit the backstreets, headlights low
Touch the brakes; No, you're too old;
Look like the wife all used and done.
I like 'em tight. I like 'em young.

Dawn peaks over scrap yards full of cars
burnt out, she heads past iron mountains,
turns for home. Mind blank; body remembering.

Andy Croft Introduces Gordon McInnes

Andy Croft lives in Middlesbrough. Among his books are *Red Letter Days, Out of the Old Earth, Selected Poems of Randall Swingler, A Weapon in the Struggle, Comrade Heart, Holme and Away* and thirty-four books for teenagers, mostly about football. His books of poetry include *Nowhere Special, Gaps Between Hills* (with Mark Robinson), *Headland, Just as Blue, Great North* and *Comrade Laughter*. He has edited three anthologies of poetry, *Red Sky at Night* (with Adrian Mitchell), *North by North East* (with Cynthia Fuller) and *Not Just a Game* (with Sue Dymoke). He runs Smokestack Books.

'Gordon McInnes and I met on two occasions to discuss his submissions to 'The Wilds'. We also exchanged several versions by e-mail. Gordon writes with terrific precision and economy, vivid miniatures of landscape, place, weather and feeling. He knows how to 'frame' a poem with just enough information. Because the poems seemed to me to be substantially finished, our discussions concentrated on small but crucial issues like line-length and line-breaks. Although the changes which Gordon subsequently made to the poems may seem small, each was the result of much discussion and each has helped to open up the narrative structure of the poems. I believe that Gordon has reached the stage where he should be sending poems out to magazines with the view to putting together his first collection.'

Gordon McInnes was born in Scotland but moved to England at a young age. His work explores dislocation and identity, particularly through the context of man in relation to natural settings, especially coastal environments. He has been published in magazines such as *KENAZ* and Interpoetry as well as being an active 'live' reader.

'It was a real help to get such detailed and constructive feedback from such an excellent reader. As an experience I found it an invaluable aid in the development of those works, particularly with reference to identifying the weak points and exploring opportunities. I feel I was able to develop 'another level' of understanding about my work - a much greater awareness of how it may impact when read for the first time.'

Lesson

'I will work hard,' said the boy,
'I will wait for you,' said his mother,
'I will shoot you,' hissed the bullet.

'I will keep you warm,' said the wall,
'I will keep you dry,' said the roof,
'I will burn you,' roared the fire.

'I will help you,' said the teacher,
'I will be your friend,' said the girl,
'I will crush you,' cried the ruins.

'I will make you smile,' said the funny drawing,
'I will make you jump,' said the basket-ball hoop,
'I will bury you,' whispered the blood.

'I will rescue you,' said the soldier,
'I will be strong,' said the president,
'I will be stronger,' said the voice in the dark.

And the world span round like a basket-ball,
And everyone did as they said they would,
And children, teachers, friends, roof, wall,
Met bullets, ruins, fire and blood.

And when it came to a stop inside the hall
The world understood the difference between
The promises that we really mean
And those which mean nothing at all.

Written On The 81

Watching an unfolding ticket
And discover in a mantra
The pitch of revving engine,
The dusty lurk of bus smell,
Stale undertones of petrol;
I'm inwardly vibrating
With the cold of organs aching
And the numb of dull gears changing
Until the whip of sudden braking,

Jars me from a stupor,

Shakes me into waking,
Distracts me from the adverts
And the shared sub-text of small talk
To see a message smeared by fingers
Condense upon the window.
It fades with age completely –
"I think my wife will leave me..."

All Flesh is Grass

I picture them breaking her ribs, just left
of the sternum, surgeons 'working' on our
baby and I want to beg them: *'Take care!'*
on returning to this Dene still unsure

of death. Yes I name it, and see a corpse
lie washed and drained of blood, gripped
in a long held pause – this rigor mortis
where I wonder when her heart was stopped.

Some places take emotion, it lives on
a residual taint, here I face it –
first fear then eventual victory.

Here in Jesmond, by the Freeman, a place
where life and death are both met with the same
small annunciation of a child's name.